LEARNING TO
Trust

Developing Confidence In God
by Bernie May

Wycliffe

LEARNING TO TRUST
© 1998 by Wycliffe Bible Translators
First Wycliffe printing July 1998
Second Wycliffe printing July 2003

©1971 by Tyndale House Publishers, Wheaton, Ill.

Verses marked TLB are from the Living Bible,

Cover Design by Jewel A. Fink

Printed in the United States of America

ISBN 0-88070-087-4

Learning to Trust

"If you want favor with both God and man, and a reputation for good judgment and common sense, then trust the Lord completely; don't ever trust yourself."

All my technical, business, and even my religious training has been based on the ability to develop human reasoning and to trust in logical conclusions drawn from available evidence.

As an airplane pilot, from the first time I sat in the beginner's seat beside my instructor I was taught to "trust" my instruments.

"Your instincts will fool you," my instructor rightly told me. "You must learn that even though you may feel you are flying south, if your compass says you are flying east, you'd better believe it."

Later, as I took my instrument training, I was taught the dangers of trusting my feelings. Often when a plane is surrounded by swirling mist and being buffeted by strong winds, you may feel you are in a dive and be tempted to pull back on the controls. But if your instruments say you are flying level—or even climbing—you'd better believe them. To pull back on the controls might put you into a steep climb, which would cause the plane to stall, drop off in a spin, and leave you out of control.

Never trust your feelings—always trust your instruments, I was told.

In the business world I was taught to analyze a problem, consider the options, determine the risk/benefit components of each option, and determine logically the best course of action. In short, I have been trained to trust the "tried and tested" management and business formulas which are taught to all those bright young students who finish graduate school with their Master of Business Administration degrees.

The same has been true in my spiritual walk. President Lyndon Johnson used to say his favorite verse of Scripture was "Come now, let us reason together..." (Isaiah 1:18). Unfortunately, he never seemed to mention the rest of the verse, which is extremely unreasonable from an earthly point of view. ("Though your sins be as scarlet, they shall be as white as snow; though they be red like crimson, they shall be as wool.") Instead, he placed the emphasis on the word reason, especially as it applied to reasoning things out with the human mind.

While all this is good when viewed on the level of human wisdom, when it comes to the spiritual side of life, it is totally backward. Yet much of this concept of trusting in things, of trusting in self, of "reasoning" things out, flavors—even dominates—our understanding of the kingdom of God.

For instance, when I started out as a young missionary pilot, my superiors used to say with humble braggadocio, "We do our best and leave the rest to God."

The problem was, we put the emphasis on *we*. Indeed, there was a general feeling that if we did our job correctly, then God wouldn't have much to do. Yet my "best" always seemed to leave God with an unfair share of the load. The emphasis, you see, was on trusting self.

A friend recently attended a marriage seminar. He returned, elated over a new revelation. "I now understand why my marriage has always been on the verge of disaster," he said. "Before we were married, my wife had an illicit affair with a married man. She realized her mistake, repented, and asked God's forgiveness. Before we were married, she confessed this to me. I told her I forgave her, but across the years I've never trusted her. Down inside I was always afraid she might do it again. Now I see that I must trust my wife."

That's a wonderful concept. We are taught that if a wife trusts her husband and a husband trusts his wife, they will have a blissful marriage. But what will happen to that marriage if one of the partners does fail? I'm afraid the devastation caused by this betrayal of trust could send the marriage into an out-of-control tailspin even worse than that which comes when a pilot pulls back on the controls and holds on.

In a pilot's language, that's called "overcontrolling." It's the same thing that happens in a marriage when one or both partners tries to control the relationship by saying, "I trust you, therefore you'd better not let me down."

The Bible does not teach us to trust one another. If I trust anyone, regardless of who it is, I will eventually be disappointed, perhaps deeply hurt. No, I am told to trust only in God...but to love people.

Yet all of life, it seems, is based on trust. We have to trust the airline captain or we'll never board a plane. Every time we drop a letter in the mailbox, we trust the postal service to deliver that letter. When we go into surgery, we trust the doctor, the nurses, the one who administers the anesthesia, the people who handle the bandages.

Every man or woman who has ever jumped from an airplane has trusted—in the parachute, in the people who packed the parachute, even in the cloth which, he believes, will hold him up and not rip open.

Most of all, we've been taught to trust ourselves. "If you want it done right, do it yourself," worldly wise men have taught us. Based on this, we have developed a high degree of self-trust.

In short, trust is an essential factor in life.

Yet all of us sense that no one is really trustworthy. There is an old story of a father who took his young son out and stood him on the railing of the back porch. He then went down, stood on the lawn, and encouraged the little fellow to jump into his arms. "I'll catch you," the father said confidently. After a lot of coaxing, the little boy finally made the leap. When he did, the father stepped back and let the child fall to the ground. He then picked his son up, dusted him off, and dried his tears. "Let that be a lesson," he said sternly. "Don't ever trust anyone."

The story sounds cruel, but the lesson is eternal. No one is completely trustworthy, including (or should I say especially?) yourself. Therefore the Bible says: trust God alone, while forgiving and loving those who let you down.

Remember: even though life is based on the

trust factor—you cannot trust in trust. You'll be disappointed...and perhaps wounded.

We've learned we can't trust in advertising, because advertisers, who have vested interests, will lie to us in order to sell their product. All of us have trusted in equipment which hasn't been trustworthy. Despite what my flight instructor said about always trusting my compass instead of my feelings, I've found that sometimes compasses can't be trusted either. There is some evidence that the Korean Airlines 747 which was shot down by the Russians during the Cold War may have strayed off course because the crew trusted either in faulty equipment, in their own faulty nature, or in a false belief that even if they did wander off course, the very worst of people would not fire on an unarmed commercial airliner. Their trust cost the lives of a lot of people.

Even our loved ones, those who would die for us, are capable of letting us down. They don't do it deliberately, but because they are made of material which is basically flawed by sin.

The result of all this is that along with our great need to trust, we are all suspicious.

A gas station in North Carolina has a sign over the door: "IN GOD WE TRUST. EVERYBODY ELSE PAYS CASH."

I propose there is a lot of theological truth in that sign.

The owner of the gas station may not be familiar with the book of Proverbs, but I imagine he's had a lot of experience with the untrustworthiness of human nature. The man who trusts in other men will be let down (or left holding a bad check). God alone is trustworthy. Trust God, love men.

"If you want favor with both God and man, and a reputation for good judgment and common sense, then trust the Lord completely: don't ever trust yourself. In everything you do, put God first, and he will direct you and crown your efforts with success" (Proverbs 3:4–6).

Don't ever trust yourself, the writer of Proverbs says. I find that difficult because I've always put a lot of trust in myself. Instead, he says, we should trust God. We all want to do that, but more and more I'm discovering just how difficult it is.

Years ago when God invaded my life, I responded by telling Him I intended to trust Him completely. That was a great statement. But it wasn't entirely true. What I was actually saying was, "I'm going to trust You—but I'm also going to trust in myself as well."

As I examine that commitment, I realize that at the time I simply wasn't able to trust fully in God. Built into me were too many reasons for trusting in myself as well. I was saying that I was going to share my trust with God. In short, I'd do my best (which I thought was pretty good) and let God take care of the deficiencies. That kind of partial trust in God wasn't based on a lack of desire, only a lack of ability to fully trust Him.

You have to learn to trust God. Trust is not a gift, like faith is. It's a learned trait. Just as we learn to distrust human nature because we've been disappointed by people who have let us down, just as we've learned the hard way that no piece of equipment is fully trustworthy, even as we have come to the painful realization that our own reasoning will let us down, so we have to learn to trust God.

Saying I'm going to trust God is like a forty-year-old man who has taken up jogging after a sedentary life saying, "Now that I started jogging yesterday, I'm going to run in the Boston Marathon next Saturday."

This poor fellow might have a great desire to run the Boston Marathon. In his badly deluded state of mind he may even think he is capable of doing it. But until a lot of things have changed in his body, he'll never make it. Oh, he might start— but he'll never complete the first mile, much less finish. His legs, his lungs, his heart—they just won't hold up. He's going to have to enter a period of training. He has to lose sixty pounds, condition his muscles, learn how to breathe correctly, change his dietary habits, get the right kind of clothes and shoes, exercise daily, and train, train, train.

At the same time he must study. He's got to find out what marathon running is all about. He has to go over the course, walking at first, then jogging, to familiarize himself with the hills, curves, and obstacles. He needs to talk to people who have run the marathon before him. Simply wanting to run it isn't good enough. He has to work at it.

Just so, the man or woman who is determined to trust God has to learn to trust God. It will take time—and training. They must learn how it is done, through trial, error, bloodied knees, and much practice.

The songwriter has caught the concept:

"Learning to lean,

Learning to lean, I'm learning to lean on Jesus.

I'm finding more power than I've ever dreamed,

I'm learning to lean on Jesus."

The secret is the learning.

Much of the problem lies in what we have to unlearn. Not only have we been taught to trust in others, in our equipment, and in ourselves, but we've picked up distorted concepts of God along the way. We've been taught—more subjectively than objectively—that God cannot be trusted fully in all matters. Perhaps God can handle big things, such as the end of the world or the ultimate outcome of good over evil, but when it comes to relatively minor things—like providing enough money for us to live on—well, we're not so sure we can trust Him in these matters.

For forty years Eunice Pike worked with the Mazatec Indians in southwestern Mexico. During this time she discovered some interesting things about these beautiful people. For instance, the people seldom wish someone well. Not only that, they are hesitant to teach one another or to share the Gospel with each other. If asked, "Who taught you to bake bread?" the village baker answers, "I just know," meaning he has acquired the knowledge without anyone's help.

Eunice says this odd behavior stems from the Indians' concept of "limited good." They believe there is only so much good, so much knowledge, so much love to go around. To teach another means you might drain yourself of knowledge. To love a second child means you have to love the first child less. To wish someone well—"Have a good day"—means you have just given away some of your own happiness, which cannot be reacquired.

A lot of Christians seem to think this way, too. They trust God, but deep down inside they suspect He's not an unlimited resource. True, they believe

God owns the cattle on a thousand hills, but they suspect His herd may be running thin. After all, a lot of people are still eating beef these days. They're afraid there's only so much money in God's coffers. If they give God's money away, it will soon be gone. They want to trust, but they have been taught that God is like man—stingy, disinterested, and surely with limits on His resources. Things like lovingkindness, mercy, and His willingness to forgive—not to mention His ability to meet our needs—are all limited. If we press God too much, we just might get the back of His hand across our face. Therefore, we need to exercise discretion in what we talk to Him about—and in how much we can actually trust Him.

But the more I study the Scriptures, the more I realize God's ways are not our ways. God's thinking is not our thinking. Our way is to trust self, not trust God. Our way is to be in control, not turn the controls over to God.

The slogan that came out of World War II sums it up: GOD IS MY CO-PILOT. In other words, I'm captain of this ship. It's under my control. God is welcome aboard; in fact, I'm delighted to have Him sit in the co-pilot's seat in case there's an emergency. But I'll not call on Him until I need Him, and even then I want Him to remember I'm still in command.

This need to unlearn applies to our ministries

as well as our personal lives. Even here (or is it "especially here," since in ministry we apply the corporate thinking of a lot of people who think God is limited) it is our abilities which need training. We have church committee meetings, mission board meetings where we sit and plan what we believe God wants to accomplish. We analyze, consider from every angle, use the counsel of men, and make judgments which we feel are God's will for our program. But we're really trusting ourselves. We trust our ability to take a certain business formula and apply it to the kingdom of God to raise money, to recruit volunteers, to build a mailing list, to increase attendance, to enlist workers, to ensure monthly donations.

And, interestingly enough, many of these methods work. But the question continues to haunt me: what if we took all our abilities and laid them humbly on the altar and simply trusted God? I believe if we did, we would move into an entirely new realm of experience.

But do we dare risk it? To do so means we have to assume that God is entirely trustworthy, that He knows what is best for us, that He will not let us down but will provide exactly what we need to get the job done in His way and in His time.

There is another promise which needs to be applied at this point. It's found in Psalm 37:5. "Trust in Him and He will act" (NEB).

Our approach is usually just the other way around. We act, and then trust God to clean up our mess or take care of the deficiencies. But the psalmist puts it in the proper perspective. Trust God and HE will act.

I am forever amazed over the ability of God to take seemingly disjointed events and put them together for His glory when men and women trust Him.

I remember being called out of a meeting in Oklahoma to take an urgent phone message from Forrey Zander, who directed the regional office of Wycliffe Bible Translators in Chicago. Forrey was excited. He had been talking with a young woman from Asia who had just completed her master's degree in communications at Wheaton College. Since foreign missionaries are no longer allowed in her country, this young woman, Thangi, had planned to return to her homeland in some missionary capacity.

Asia is a vast continent with many diverse cultures and languages. Thangi's parents, who are national missionaries, work near an area where more than half a million people represent twenty different languages and dialects. Only two language groups have portions of the Scripture. Her father, knowing she was about to graduate from Wheaton, had asked her to consider returning home as a Bible translator.

Thangi had contacted Forrey in our Chicago office. He, in turn, had suggested she apply to the Summer Institute of Linguistics school in Dallas—to work on another master's degree, this time in linguistics. It was now one week before deadline and Thangi was still $1,000 short. Forrey was calling, asking if I could raise the money for this critical need.

I had just come out of a meeting with a number of representatives from various divisions of Wycliffe Bible Translators. They had come from many different parts of the world to present their financial needs—which totaled more than eight million dollars. Some of these needs had been critical for years. Now Forrey was asking me to put Thangi at the front of the line.

I knew I had the ability to raise the money. I knew I could bypass the request from Indonesia to raise thirty-three thousand dollars to buy a new electrical generator to give power to the jungle base at Danau Bira. I could bypass the need to find money to purchase a new airplane to replace the one which had recently crashed in South America. Sure there was enough money—in some budget category—to send Thangi to graduate school in Dallas so she could return home as a Bible translator to her own people. All I would have to do was to change some priorities. But I also knew that that would be trusting in my own ability. I felt God was asking me to trust Him.

"I can't treat her in a special way," I told Forrey. "But if God wants her in school this week, we can trust Him to locate and provide the funds. I will do two things. I'll pray about it. And if anyone approaches me and says they have one thousand dollars to help train a national translator, I'll direct the money to Thangi."

I could hear the air escaping from Forrey's punctured balloon. But since he also understands what it means to trust God and not self, he agreed to my terms. He contacted Thangi, told her of the decision to trust God, and received her enthusiastic approval. She, too, understood the principle.

The next day I had lunch with a wealthy man who could have easily written out a check for one thousand dollars to send Thangi to school. All I had to do was use some marketing and sales ability I had learned a long time ago and I knew he would give me the money. But I had no leading to ask for money for Thangi. I left the luncheon feeling guilty, but I knew it was right to wait on God.

Two days later I was flying my plane from Oklahoma back to California. The weather was bad over the southern route, so I flew home by way of Colorado. I knew my friends, Henry and Marcia Stuart from Dallas, were probably vacationing in their cabin near Crested Butte. I needed gas anyway, so when I stopped over, I gave them a call.

Henry was delighted to hear my voice and drove over and picked me up at the airport to take me out to his house. I was just getting ready to sit down on the porch and drink a glass of tea when Henry spoke up.

"Bernie, I'm glad you stopped by. I've been thinking about the work carried on by Wycliffe Bible Translators. It seems you ought to try to find some Christian nationals and begin training them to help with Bible translation. If you ever find anyone like that, I'd like to invest one thousand dollars to help with their education."

I began to laugh. "Let me tell you about Thangi," I said. By the time I had finished my story, Marcia had brought Henry the checkbook and I had the money in hand.

I borrowed Henry's phone and called Forrey in Chicago. He in turn called Thangi, who saw it as a confirmation of God's will. Flying on to California, I filled the cockpit with praise to our God who takes loose ends and weaves a beautiful tapestry. A young Indian woman at Wheaton had opened her life to God's call—trusted Him to act. A father back in India who sensed a need trusted God and spoke what he believed was the word of the Lord to his daughter. Our Chicago Wycliffe executive had communicated that need to me and trusted God to act. A Texas couple, vacationing in Colorado with some of God's money in their pocket, trusted God to act and to show them where He wanted the money. And then there was me. We were all trusting God—and He acted.

There is no way man can engineer something like this. God, however, has a plan for every life. Where there is a plan, there is a purpose behind it. And with every purpose and plan, there is ample provision. All God needs are men and women who will not lean on their own understanding, but will trust Him. Some years ago I was executive director of JAARS, the transportation and communication arm of Wycliffe Bible Translators. We were then operating fifty airplanes in thirteen countries, serving pioneer ministries, Bible translators, and literacy workers. It was a big responsibility. We worked hard and took seriously the task God had given us.

The early '70s produced a great interest and increase in helicopter technology as a result of the Vietnam war. Thousands of young men had been trained as pilots. They served in Vietnam and then returned to the United States. Many of these men were Christians, wondering what God wanted them to do with their lives. A number of them contacted us at JAARS, asking why mission organizations like ours weren't interested in using helicopters.

Both JAARS and a sister organization, Mission Aviation Fellowship (MAF)—as well as other mission groups who used airplanes—had been considering the use of helicopters. But all of us had run tests, analyzed things from a business and practical standpoint, and concluded that while helicopters would indeed be a great help to us, it was impossible to utilize them. Our statistical analysis at JAARS, for instance, indicated that the cost of purchasing, operating, and maintaining helicopters was far too great for our budget. In fact, even though the marvelous machines would be of great help in the jungle, it would cost four times as much to transport cargo via helicopter as it did via single engine airplanes. Furthermore, maintenance was very high on helicopters. Payload was low. Range was short. Our conclusion: it was impractical.

That, however, was man's conclusion based on trusting man's ability to analyze a situation and come up with a reasonable answer.

About that time I made a trip to the island of Papua New Guinea. Papua New Guinea has been one of our largest and most challenging mission fields. More than seven hundred different languages are spoken there. Many of the people do not have a written language—no alphabet, no books, no way of communicating through writing, and of course not a single Bible in their own language. Wycliffe Bible Translators and a number of other mission groups are working diligently to change that situation.

While in Papua New Guinea, I met a young translator and his wife, Neil and Carol Anderson, who approached me after I had spoken to a large group of missionaries at a highland center. Carol explained how God had called them to a remote mountain village. To get to their village, they had to fly by small plane to a jungle airstrip and then hike for three days up a precarious mountain trail. The razorsharp shale and rocks on the trail totally destroyed a pair of hiking boots each trip they made. Furthermore, the leeches were so thick that the Andersons had to stop every few hours to pull the blood-sucking creatures off their skin. They always arrived in their village cut and bruised and on the verge of exhaustion. Very sweetly Carol asked if it would ever be possible for JAARS to provide a helicopter to help them get to their mountaintop village.

I immediately began explaining how our research on helicopters had shown us it was impractical and economically impossible to give it consideration. She accepted my reasoning graciously, but as she turned and walked away, something deep inside of me reacted. It was as though I heard God say, "You've worked on this problem and come to some very reasonable conclusions. But you've never asked me about it."

What Neil and Carol Anderson were doing with their lives was not logical. It was not "reasonable" for a brilliant young couple to carry the Gospel to that dismal, remote spot. Yet they had not considered the reasonableness of it—they had simply asked God, received an answer, and responded. I determined to seek God further in the matter.

Returning to our JAARS headquarters in North Carolina, I called a staff meeting and suggested we pray about the possibility of using helicopters. Immediately my staff members began to respond. They reminded me we had already considered this in great detail, had done much research, and had concluded it was impractical. I responded that I knew all that, but it was just possible God knew something we didn't know.

We had our prayer meeting, opening ourselves to God and asking Him to show us if it was His will for us to move out into an area that was beyond our thinking. Should we use helicopters?

The next day I received a letter from a man in California. His name was Jim Burroughs. An aircraft helicopter mechanic, working in Bakersfield, he was an expert in repairing damaged helicopters. Recently he and his wife, along with a small group of Christians, had purchased a damaged helicopter. They had rebuilt it and now wanted to donate it to a missionary organization.

He had written another missionary organization and had received from them the same answer he would have gotten from us had he written before our prayer meeting. But we had said we were going to trust God—believing He would act. Was it possible Jim Burroughs's letter was an "act of God"? I figured the only way to find out was by telling him we were willing to pursue the matter further.

I had already planned to make a trip to California, so when I got there I went by to see Jim. I knew if we were going to start using helicopters we would need a lot more than one. I told Jim we'd probably have to settle for machines which had been damaged and that meant we'd need a man like him to put them in first-class condition. He responded, "If God provides the helicopters, I'll move to Waxhaw and overhaul them."

I knew the military had hundreds of used helicopters that were being brought back home from Vietnam. I had seen thousands of them in Saigon at the air base there. I checked around and discovered that many of these machines were stored at Davis-Monthan Air Force Base in Tucson, Arizona. On my way back from California I stopped in Tucson and was escorted through the air base, where I saw hundreds of excess government helicopters sitting in rows a half-mile long. The government, it seemed, had no plans for them. Yet the question remained: Even if we had some of them, could we afford to keep them?

The following week I went to Washington, where I met with a government official. I had determined to pursue the matter as long as God kept the door open. The official was hostile, but as I told him of Neil and Carol Anderson, he began to soften. When I finished, he said, "Mister, how many helicopters do you want?"

I had expected God to act—but not that quickly. Without really thinking, I said, "If we could just get six of those used helicopters at Davis-Monthan...."

"No," he objected. "You don't want those. They're old ones. We have some new ones that will become surplus in a couple of months in Hawaii. All you have to do is get the serial numbers of six of those helicopters and I'll designate them for your work."

I walked out of his office, staggered by the rapidity with which God worked once I trusted Him. I called my friend Bob Burdick, a captain for United Airlines, and told him I needed the serial numbers off of six helicopters in Hawaii. The next day Bob flew on United Airlines to Hawaii and got the numbers, and three days later I was back in the official's office in Washington, D.C. His response was, "You certainly have an efficient organization."

When God acts on our trust, I discovered, He acts big. The next few months revealed miracle after miracle. Not only did we have pilots and mechanics begin to apply for positions, but the government called back and said that they were phasing out that particular model of helicopter, and they gave us more than one million dollars' worth of extra engines and spare parts, plus seven more helicopters. Before we knew it, we were in the helicopter business with thirteen machines and more parts than we could store.

After we put our first helicopters on the field, we ran a cost analysis program. We discovered that because of all God had done, we could fly cargo in the helicopter for the same price we had been hauling it in our single-engine airplanes— exactly one-quarter our original estimate. Jim Burroughs and his wife moved to our center at Waxhaw, North Carolina, and he became our first helicopter mechanic. Because of all these events, Neil and Carol Anderson can now reach their tribal people in minutes rather than days. And shortly afterward, many other missionary organizations which use aircraft also began using helicopters, making the work much easier and more efficient.

All this has taught me a few things about trusting God.

One: No matter how well I plan, God's way is going to be something different. Proverbs says, "We can make our plans, but the final outcome is in God's hands" (Proverbs 16:1). Another verse says it even stronger: "Since the Lord is directing our steps, why try to understand everything that happens along the way?" (Proverbs 20:24).

I've never had a plan that has worked out just like I planned it. God has always had something different in mind. All I need to do is trust Him and take the steps that are open. He does the rest.

Two: God's ways are always best. If you become too enthralled with your own plans, you'll be disappointed when they don't work out.

I remember the time we were getting ready to send a helicopter to the Philippines. For two years we had been making plans. The pilot had struggled to raise his financial support, to finish his training, and to get all his affairs in order so he could move to the Philippines. The helicopter was to be shipped in a huge crate on an ocean freighter. We were just crating it up—and the pilot was leaving that morning—when I received a telegram. Our field committee in the Philippines had changed their minds. What a disappointment! We had been working on this project for two years. The pilot had made his plans. Now all that seemed to be dashed on the rocks of disappointment.

But God gave us all special grace to trust Him. Two weeks later we received an urgent request from Indonesia. They desperately needed a helicopter. If we could ship one immediately, the government—which recognized the need because of a recent earthquake—would grant permission for its entrance, a process that often takes years. I began to laugh. It just so happened we had a helicopter sitting in a crate—and a qualified pilot ready to go with it.

Two years later our folks in the Philippines were ready for their helicopter. God had delayed their request because He knew a door was about to open in Indonesia. God's ways are always best.

Three: God will accomplish His purposes whether we cooperate or not.

Missionary work, for instance, has gone forward by both the voluntary and the involuntary actions of God's people. The dispersal of the church in the first century was God's way of speeding up the spread of the gospel to the ends of the earth. Later, God allowed the barbarians of the north to overrun the Roman Empire, which allowed the Gospel to penetrate an unknown world. The captivity and martyrdom of God's people has done more to spread the Gospel than all of man's efforts combined. God will accomplish His purposes—because they are His.

Finally: I have learned that trusting God is my own way to personal growth. I think of the thousands of missionaries who have been sent out through Wycliffe Bible Translators, thinking their sole purpose was to translate the Bible into the languages of Bibleless people groups. Invariably so many of these people return and say the greatest thing which happened to them was not completing the translation of the Bible—as monumental a task as that is—but the fact that as they trusted God for this impossible task, they found themselves actually growing into the image of Jesus Christ.

That, it seems, is the ultimate reason for trust. Not that we trust God for some task, or some provision, or some purpose—but that we trust Him because He is God. And as we trust, we come to know Him, to love Him, and to grow into His likeness.

And that is the greatest miracle of all.